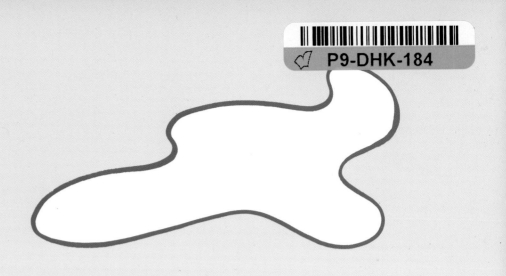

OR DIE

How Thirteen States Became a Nation

Illustrated by

Jef Czekaj

HOW EXCITING!

iⁱⁱⁱi Charlesbridge

On September 3, 1783, the Treaty of Paris

was signed, officially ending the American Revolution. Thirteen colonies had won their independence from England. A new country was born.

George Washington, the commander of the Continental army, said good-bye to his troops and went back to his home, Mount Vernon, in Virginia.

The new country was called the United States of America—but it was not united. Each state had its own leaders and its own government. The states were like thirteen separate countries.

The country operated under a document called the Articles of Confederation. This political system gave the national government very little power. Each state took care of its own business without interference or help from anyone.

But being thirteen independent states had its drawbacks. Without a strong national government, it wasn't easy for the states to trade with one another or with foreign countries.

11

There was no one to settle disagreements over borders and trade. There was no one to provide help if a state was in trouble.

The convention began on May 25, 1787.

Twelve states sent delgates.

There were fifty-five delegates in all, including some of
the most brilliant minds in the country: James Madison,
Alexander Hamilton, Roger Sherman, George Mason,
George Washington, and Benjamin Franklin. Thomas
Jefferson and John Adams were in Europe, however,
serving as ambassadors.

As president of the convention, George Washington sat in a beautiful carved chair. He had a front-row seat for all the arguments.

Doors were locked and guards were stationed outside. There were no meetings with the press. The delegates were serious about keeping their conversations private.

21

The smaller states counterattacked by presenting the New Jersey Plan.

The big states and the small states argued for weeks. Delegates became discouraged. George Washington looked haggard, as if he were reliving the terrible days at Valley Forge.

A major hurdle had been overcome. The delegates now had a framework for a new constitution. But there were still many other decisions to be made.

The powers among the executive, legislative, and judicial branches were carefully separated and balanced in the new constitution. For instance, the president can veto a law passed by Congress. Congress can remove a president from office if he misbehaves. Only Congress, not the president, can declare war. And the judicial branch has the power to settle disagreements between the other branches.

Because it would be nearly impossible to get unanimous approval for all changes, the Constitution says amendments become law if ratified (formally accepted) by three-fourths of the states.

The final section of the Constitution, Article VII, says that the document would become law when nine out of the thirteen states ratified it.

So, we're finished.

Yup! It's time to get this ball rolling! Who will be the first to sign?

DE

George Washington, of course!

37

On September 17, 1787,

the United States Constitution was signed by representatives of twelve states. The ratification process was lengthy, but eventually all thirteen states approved the Constitution— even Rhode Island. A new government was born.

The United States of America!

United at last and ready to govern ourselves!

Afterword

The Constitutional Convention took place in Philadelphia during the hot summer of 1787. Its purpose was to revise the existing Articles of Confederation, to solve the many problems among the states. But the Articles of Confederation were so weak that the delegates soon realized they would need to come up with a completely new government to be successful. Fifty-five men from Massachusetts, Virginia, Georgia, North Carolina, South Carolina, New Hampshire, New York, Maryland, Delaware, Pennsylvania, New Jersey, and Connecticut met in secret for four months.

One of the largest debates focused on representation. When the states agreed to the compromise presented by the Connecticut delegation, it was a turning point. A congress with two parts, having equal representation in the Senate and representation based on population in the House of Representatives, solved one big problem. But there were other controversies and many important decisions. How should the president be elected? The document the delegates created carefully separated and balanced power among the executive, legislative, and judicial branches of government. This system of "checks and balances" ensured that no one branch of the government could take complete control.

The Constitution contains many specifics, such as how old our legislators must be to run for office, what the powers of Congress are, and how Supreme Court justices are selected. But the fifty-five white male delegates also created a document that could expand to serve a society not yet imagined in 1787. By including an amendment process, they acknowledged that the Constitution might need adjustments in the future. The voting rights of African American men were not guaranteed by the Constitution until the Fifteenth Amendment was passed in 1870. Women did not obtain the right to vote until the Nineteenth Amendment in 1920. The Constitution was ingeniously designed as a living document, creating a government capable of serving Americans from generation to generation.

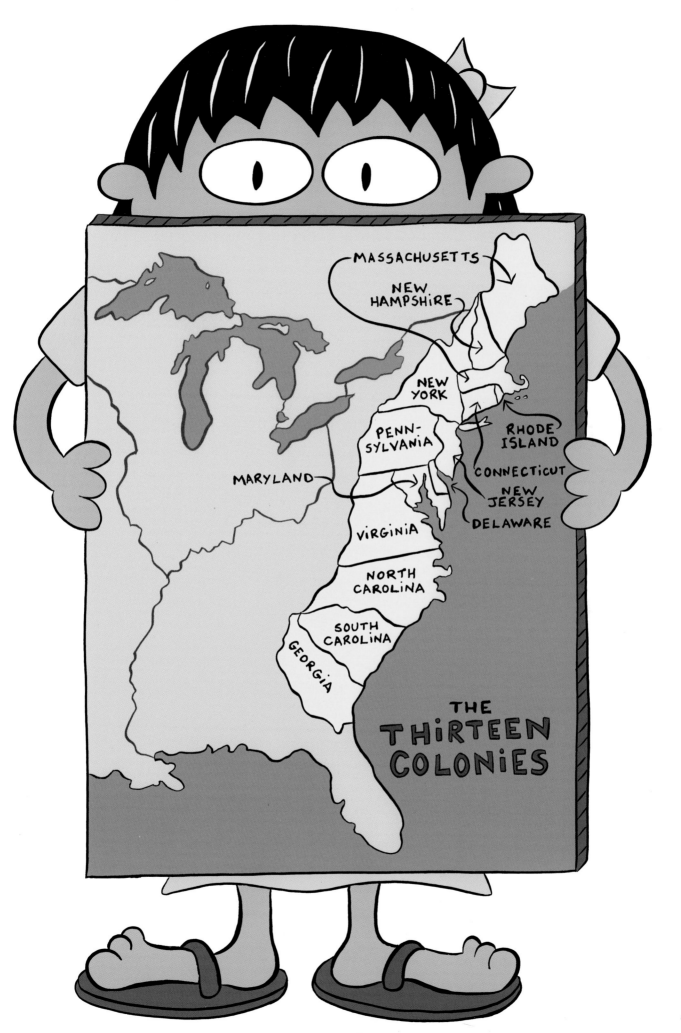

Notes

Page 9. Why wasn't the country united?

The Articles of Confederation stated: "The stile of this confederacy shall be 'The United States of America.'" But loyalty to the United States as a country was not firmly established. Most people considered themselves citizens of their particular states. The Articles of Confederation established only "a league of friendship" among the states, rather than a strong government with a leader.

Page 11. Who printed the money?

While the country operated under the Articles of Confederation, every state printed its own money. Traveling from one state to another was like visiting another country. The money was different, and so was the government. This contributed to economic and trade difficulties in the new country.

Pages 12-13. Who owned Vermont?

The land that later became Vermont was claimed by both New Hampshire and New York. Many states had border conflicts. Maryland and Virginia fought over rights on the Potomac River. Without a strong central government, the states were like a squabbling family.

Page 12. Who was Daniel Shays?

Daniel Shays, a farmer and Revolutionary War veteran, was the leader of a yearlong rebellion in Massachusetts that began in the summer of 1786. The farmers were angry over high taxes and farm foreclosures. Armed with pitchforks and muskets, they closed down courthouses and attempted to take over the arsenal in Springfield, Massachusetts. The state government eventually crushed the rebellion, but the situation pointed out the need for a stronger federal government that could help states in times of crisis.

Pages 14-15. Why was Annapolis important?

The Annapolis Convention in 1786 was supposed to be a meeting of all thirteen states, but only delegates from Pennsylvania, Delaware, Virginia, New Jersey, and New York came. Even Maryland, the state where the convention was held, didn't send delegates. While the original purpose was to solve trade issues between the states, the meeting identified the weakness of the Articles of Confederation as the overriding problem. The men at Annapolis decided to call another convention with the express purpose of strengthening the Articles of Confederation. A meeting that only decides to hold another meeting may not appear to be much of a success. But this decision laid the foundation for the writing of the Constitution.

Pages 17-19. What about those special chairs?

Benjamin Franklin did travel to Independence Hall in a sedan chair carried on poles by four men. At eighty-one years old, his health was poor, and it was too painful for him to ride in a carriage.

The back of George Washington's chair was decorated with a half sun. Franklin said he contemplated this design throughout the convention, wondering if it was a rising sun or a setting sun. At the end of the convention, when the Constitution was signed, Franklin was happy to report that Washington's chair was adorned with a rising sun, a symbol of promise for the future.

Pages 18-19. Why did they keep everything secret?

The delegates agreed right away on two things: they wanted George Washington to preside over the convention, and they wanted the proceedings to be kept private. Secrecy meant that the delegates could discuss the issues freely without worrying about the reaction of the press or the public. They were also free to change their minds. Some believe that secrecy was one of the keys to success. The rule was strictly enforced. Delegates kept a discreet eye on Benjamin Franklin, who loved to talk, making sure that he did not let any news slip unintentionally during a dinner conversation.

So how do we know what happened behind those closed doors if the press was not allowed to report on a day-to-day basis? James Madison, a Virginia delegate who later became president, attended every session and took careful notes of the proceedings. These notes are a primary source of much of our information about the convention. He sponsored the Virginia Plan, which began the discussion of a new constitution. For his role as a leading figure at the convention, he was nicknamed "the Father of the Constitution."

Pages 26-27. Why did George Washington look so glum?

The issue of representation created a stalemate. Some delegates worried that the convention would break up. Benjamin Franklin called for prayer. And George Washington looked discouraged, the way he did at Valley Forge, one of the lowest points of the Revolutionary War. As president of the convention, Washington was largely silent. But his presence was extremely important. Washington had come out of retirement to show his support for a strong national government.

Pages 28-29. How did Roger Sherman save the day?

Roger Sherman, one of the delegates from Connecticut, is often credited with presenting the Great Compromise, also known as the Connecticut Compromise. This plan took advantage of a bicameral legislature, a congress with two houses. Under this system, every piece of legislation is discussed and voted on by two different legislative bodies. It must be passed by both houses before becoming law. Bicameral legislatures were common in 1787. England's parliament was composed of the House of Lords and the House of Commons. Many of the individual states had bicameral legislatures. Sherman's plan proposed that every state, regardless of size, have two representatives in an upper house, the Senate, and representation based on population in a lower house, the House of Representatives. It was a compromise that gave both the states and the people power.

Pages 32-33. Who does what?

The careful separation of powers among the branches of government even extends to the duties of the Senate and the House of Representatives. The House has the sole authority to introduce laws for raising taxes, and to choose a president if no candidate receives the majority of the electoral votes. The Senate has the sole power to ratify treaties and approve presidential appointees, such as Supreme Court justices. If an official is suspected of wrongdoing, the House can vote to impeach him or her. It is then the Senate's responsibility to serve as a court to convict or acquit the accused official. Members of the House of Representatives serve a two-year term, and senators serve a six-year term.

Page 34. How many things have been changed?

There have been twenty-seven amendments to the Constitution. Some of them modified governmental procedures. For example, the Constitution originally said that the person who received the second largest number of votes in the Electoral College—the runner-up— would be the vice president. This proved impractical with the advent of political parties and was changed with the Twelfth Amendment, ratified in 1804. Today, Americans vote for a president and a vice president.

Pages 38-39. What about Rhode Island?

Not only did Rhode Island refuse to attend the Constitutional Convention, it was the last state to ratify the Constitution. Rhode Island held an anti-federalist opinion that a strong central government would rob states of their individual rights. Those opposed to the Constitution were also disappointed that it had no protection for the individual freedoms of citizens. In response to this criticism, the first ten amendments, known as the Bill of Rights, were added in 1791. Rhode Island joined the union in 1790, two years after the Constitution went into effect.

Rights make it right! I'm in.

RI

Read the Constitution for yourself!

www.archives.gov/national-archives-experience/charters/constitution.html

Bibliography

American Political Science Association. *This Constitution: From Ratification to the Bill of Rights.* Washington, DC: Congressional Quarterly, 1988.

Collier, Christopher, and James Lincoln Collier. *Creating the Constitution, 1787.* New York: Benchmark Books, 1999.

Colman, Warren. *The Constitution.* Chicago: Children's Press, 1987.

Conley, Patrick T., and John P. Kaminski, eds. *The Constitution and the States.* Madison, WI: Madison House, 1988.

Finkelman, Paul. *The Constitution.* Washington, DC: National Geographic, 2006.

Fradin, Dennis Brindell. *The Founders: The 39 Stories Behind the U.S. Constitution.* New York: Walker & Co., 2005.

Fritz, Jean. *Shh! We're Writing the Constitution.* New York: Scholastic, 1987.

Hakim, Joy. *A History of US: From Colonies to Country.* New York: Oxford University Press, 2005.

Horn, Geoffrey. *The Constitution.* Milwaukee, WI: World Almanac Library, 2004.

Levy, Elizabeth. *If You Were There When They Signed the Constitution.* New York: Scholastic, 1987.

Lomask, Milton. *The Spirit of 1787.* New York: Farrar, Straus & Giroux, 1980.

Maestro, Betsy, and Giulio Maestro. *A More Perfect Union.* New York: Lothrop, Lee & Shepherd, 1987.

McPhillips, Martin. *The Constitutional Convention.* Morristown, NJ: Silver Burdett, 1985.

Mee, Charles. *The Genius of the People.* New York: Harper & Row, 1987.

Moyers, Bill. *Moyers: Report from Philadelphia.* New York: Ballantine Books, 1987.

Prolman, Marilyn. *The Constitution.* Chicago: Children's Press, 1995.

Quiri, Patricia Ryon. *The Constitution.* New York: Children's Press, 1998.

Sgroi, Peter. *This Constitution.* New York: Franklin Watts, 1986.

For my son, Neal—J. J.

For Kyle Czekaj—J. C.

Text copyright © 2009 by Jacqueline Jules
Illustrations copyright © 2009 by Jef Czekaj

Published by Charlesbridge
85 Main Street
Watertown, MA 02472
(617) 926-0329
www.charlesbridge.com

Library of Congress Cataloging-in-Publication Data
Jules, Jacqueline, 1956–
    Unite or die : how thirteen states became a nation / Jacqueline Jules ;
illustrated by Jef Czekaj.
        p. cm.
    Includes bibliographical references.
    ISBN 978-1-58089-189-9 (reinforced for library use)
    ISBN 978-1-58089-190-5 (softcover)
    ISBN 978-1-60734-133-8 (ebook pdf)
1. United States—Politics and government—1783–1789—Juvenile literature.
2. United States. Constitution—Juvenile literature. 3. Constitutional
history—United States—Juvenile literature. 4. United States—History—
1783–1815—Juvenile literature. I. Czekaj, Jef, ill. II. Title.
E303.J85 2009
973.3—dc22   2008007229

Printed in Korea
(hc) 10 9 8 7 6 5 4 3 2 1
(sc) 10 9 8 7 6

Line art drawn in ink on Bristol and then scanned and
    colored on an Apple iBook using Adobe Photoshop 6.0
Display type set in Animated Gothic Heavy, P22 Mayflower,
    P22 Operina Corsivo, and P22 Operina Romano;
    text type set in Adobe Caslon and Blambot Pro Lite
Color separations by Chroma Graphics, Singapore
Printed by Sung In Printing in Gunpo-Si, Kyonggi-Do, Korea
Production supervision by Brian G. Walker
Designed by Jef Czekaj and Susan Mallory Sherman